KU-213-435

WHY SHOULD I LISTEN?

HODDER
Wayland

an imprint of Hodder Children's Books

WHY SHOULD I?

WHY SHOULD I Eat Well?
WHY SHOULD I Help?
WHY SHOULD I Listen?
WHY SHOULD I Share?

Published in Great Britain in 2001 by Hodder Wayland,
an imprint of Hodder Children's Books

Commissioning editor: Alex Woolf
Editor: Liz Gogerly
Designer: Jean Wheeler
Digital Colour: Carl Gordon

British Library Cataloguing in Publication Data
Llewellyn, Claire
Why should I listen?
1. Listening – Juvenile literature 2. Awareness – Juvenile literature
I. Title II. Listen
153.6'8

ISBN 0 7502 3293 5

Printed and bound in Italy by G. Canale & C.Sp.A., Turin

Hodder Children's Books
A division of Hodder Headline Limited
338 Euston Road, London NW1 3BH

WHY SHOULD I LISTEN?

Written by Claire Llewellyn

Illustrated by Mike Gordon

HODDER
Wayland

an imprint of Hodder Children's Books

I can hear wonderful things
when I really listen
... a beautiful song thrush

4

... a grasshopper
on the lawn

... and the crunch of freshly
fallen snow.

But sometimes I find it hard to listen. It's often when I'm really busy – watching TV ...

6

7

Some people ask – why should I listen?
Well ... NOT listening can get you
into trouble.

11

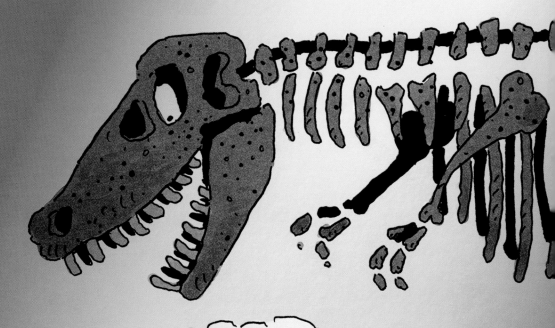

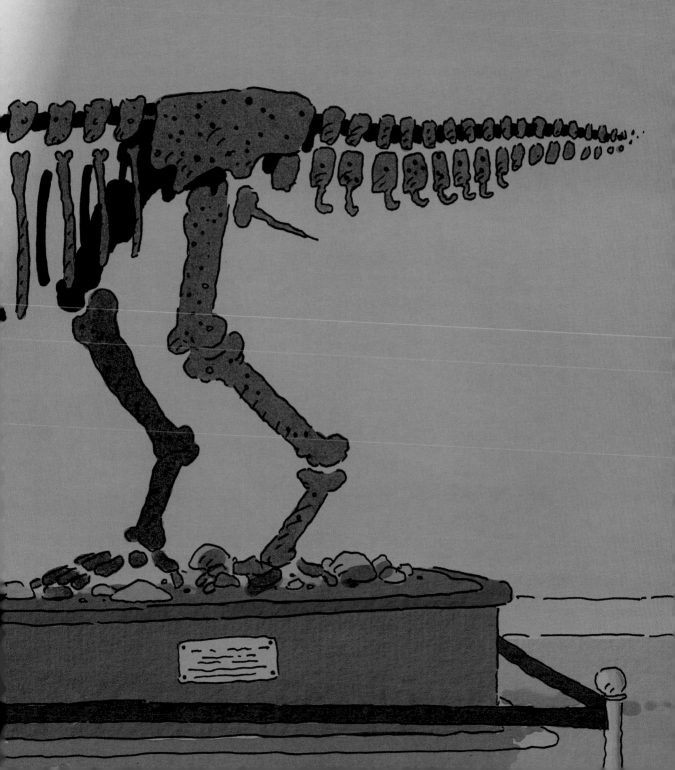

And what do you think happened at Isobel's party because I didn't hear a word she said?

Cool!

14

15

16

And guess what happened to my sister last summer, when I didn't listen to my Mum?

19

So now when someone is talking,
I'm trying very hard to listen.

27

And pick up the things
that I need to hear.

Mind the wet
paint, Joe!

You need your PE
shoes tomorrow.

28

29

Notes for parents and teachers

Why Should I? and the National Curriculum

The *Why Should I?* series satisfies a number of requirements for the *Personal, Social and Health Education non-statutory framework at Key Stage 1*. Within the category *Developing confidence and responsibility*, these books will help young readers to recognize what they like and dislike, what is fair and unfair, and what is right and wrong; to think about themselves, learn from their experiences and recognize what they are good at. Under *Developing a healthy, safer lifestyle*, some of the titles in this series will help to teach children how to make simple choices that improve their health and well-being, to maintain personal hygiene, and to learn rules for, and ways of, keeping safe, including basic road safety. Under *Developing good relationships and respecting the differences between people*, reading these books will help children to recognize how their behaviour affects other people, to listen to other people and play and work cooperatively, and that family and friends should care for each other.

About *Why Should I Listen?*

Why Should I Listen? is intended to be an enjoyable book which discusses the importance of listening. A variety of situations throughout this book explore the ways in which this vital skill can help children.

Listening helps children to play an active role in their family, their class and school. Answering a ringing phone, helping out at home and bringing things into class are all valuable tasks for young children, helping them to feel good about themselves and preparing them for greater independence and responsibility.

Listening is vital in developing relationships with others. Listening to others helps children to work together, to learn how their behaviour affects others and to share each other's feelings. Some children find it hard to think about anything outside themselves. Learning to consider others is part of growing up.

Being listened to helps children's self-esteem and enables them to be open and express their feelings. It helps them to develop an understanding and knowledge of themselves as individuals.

Listening is important in keeping safe. Listening to the people who care for them helps children to learn the basic rules and skills for keeping themselves safe. Listening out for vital information such as where it is safe to cross the road is an important step in taking some responsibility for themselves.

Suggestions as you read the book with children

The book is full of examples of times when a child has either succeeded or failed to listen. As you come across each example, it might be useful to stop and discuss it with children. When do they find it hard to listen? Why is that?

All of us sometimes fail to listen. How would they feel if they turned up at a swimming party without their costume? Has something similar ever happened to them? Talking and thinking about past disasters may help to avoid a repetition.

Being listened to is important for everyone – adults and children. Can they remember a time when they weren't listened to? Adults are often guilty of not listening to children. Why do they think this is? What could they say to an adult who wasn't listening to them?

Suggested follow-up activities

You could ask children to volunteer examples of their favourite sounds (the first cuckoo, the ice-cream man or the theme tune of their favourite TV programme) and draw pictures of them. Make a wall display under the heading 'Listen!'.

Children could write accounts, or make up stories about not listening. These could be put together to make a class book.

Take children for a walk. Before you go, ask them to predict what sounds they might hear on the walk (e.g. birdsong, an overhead plane, a dog barking etc.). Draw symbols for about ten different sounds on a piece of paper, photocopy it and give a copy to each child. While they are on the walk, ask them to tick the symbols of any of the sounds they hear (and note down any others).

Play Simon Says. In this game, one person is 'Simon' and tells the others what to do: 'Simon says, scratch your nose/touch your ear/hop on one leg' etc. Occasionally, Simon tricks the group by omitting to say the words 'Simon says' before the instruction. Anyone who follows the instruction without these words is out of the game.

Books to read

Not now, Bernard by David Mckee
(Red Fox, 1982)
A picture book about a boy
who isn't listened to.

The Boy Who Cried Wolf
by Tony Ross
(Red Fox, 1986)
The traditional story about
the boy who tricked people
into 'listening' to him, and who
consequently wasn't listened to
when it mattered.